THE COMPLETE MEDITERRANEAN DIET COOKBOOK 2024

Transform Your Lifestyle with Quick and Easy Recipes for Lasting Health and Joyful Living

Dr. Raphael Rachelle

Copyright © by Dr. Raphael Rachelle 2023. All rights reserved. Before this document is duplicated or reproduced in any manner, the publisher's consent must be gained. Therefore, the contents within can neither be stored electronically, transferred, nor kept in database.

Neither in Part nor full can the document be copied, scanned, faxed, or retained without approval from the publisher or creator.

TABLE OF CONTENTS

INTRODUCTION 11

Overview, Health Benefits and Research Findings......................13

Emphasis on Whole, Unprocessed Foods 17

Analysis of Key Nutrients and Their Impact on Health 20

Food to Include, Limit and Avoid 23

Delicious Breakfast Recipes 27

    Greek Yogurt Parfait:..27

    Mediterranean Veggie Omelet 27

    Banana and Almond Butter Toast 28

    Spinach and Feta Breakfast Wrap 28

    Overnight Chia Seed Pudding: 29

    Avocado and Smoked Salmon Bagel: 29

    Mediterranean Frittata: 30

    Blueberry and Almond Smoothie Bowl 30

    Whole Wheat Pancakes with Berries: 31

    Veggie and Cheese Breakfast Burrito: 31

Sides Recipes 32

Tzatziki Sauce: 32

Roasted Garlic and Rosemary Potatoes: 32

Greek Salad: 33

Lemon Garlic Quinoa: 34

Caprese Skewers: 34

Spinach and Feta Stuffed Mushrooms: 35

Grilled Asparagus with Lemon Zest: 35

Eggplant Caponata: 36

Quinoa Tabbouleh: 36

Mediterranean Roasted Vegetables: 37

Main Courses 38

Lemon Herb Grilled Chicken: 38

Mediterranean Baked Cod: 38

Eggplant Parmesan: 39

Mediterranean Shrimp and Orzo Salad: 40

Chicken Souvlaki Skewers: 41

Lentil and Vegetable Moussaka: 41

Spinach and Feta Stuffed Chicken Breast: 42

Grilled Vegetable and Halloumi Skewers: 43

Pasta Puttanesca 44

Stuffed Bell Peppers with Quinoa and Chickpeas: 45

Appetizers and Snacks Recipes 46

Hummus and Veggie Platter: 46

Caprese Skewers: 46

Greek Spanakopita Triangles: 47

Tomato Bruschetta: 47

Stuffed Grape Leaves (Dolma): 48

Greek Yogurt and Cucumber Dip: 49

Olive Tapenade: 49

Baked Feta with Honey and Nuts: 50

Mediterrancan Bruschetta: 50

Spicy Roasted Chickpeas: 51

Salads and Soup Recipes 52

Greek Salad: 52

Quinoa Salad with Chickpeas and Lemon Vinaigrette: 53

Mediterranean Chickpea Salad: 54

Lentil and Vegetable Soup: 55

Fattoush Salad: 56

Minestrone Soup: 57

Tabbouleh Salad: 58

Gazpacho: 59

Cretan Dakos Salad: 60

Lemon Chickpea Orzo Soup: 60

Dessert Recipes 62

Greek Yogurt and Honey Parfait: 62

Mediterranean Orange and Almond Cake: 62

Baklava: 63

Italian Tiramisu: 64

Lemon Sorbet: 64

Fig and Walnut Phyllo Rolls: 65

Orange Blossom Panna Cotta: 66

Ricotta and Honey Stuffed Figs: 66

Drizzle with additional honey and top with chopped pistachios.
.... 67

- Chocolate Olive Oil Cake: 67
- Lemon and Lavender Shortbread Cookies: 68

Smoothies Recipes 69

- Berry Blast Smoothie: 69
- Green Tropical Smoothie: 69
- Peanut Butter Banana Protein Smoothie: 70
- Citrus Sunshine Smoothie: 70
- Avocado and Kale Power Smoothie: 71
- Mango Coconut Bliss Smoothie: 71
- Blueberry Almond Spinach Smoothie: 72
- Watermelon Mint Cooler Smoothie: 73
- Chocolate Banana Almond Smoothie: 73
- Pineapple Ginger Turmeric Smoothie: 74

Vegetarian Recipes 75

- Quinoa Stuffed Bell Peppers: 75
- Eggplant Parmesan: 76
- Lentil and Vegetable Stir-Fry: 76
- Spinach and Feta Stuffed Mushrooms: 77

Chickpea and Vegetable Curry: 78

Caprese Pasta Salad: 79

Sweet Potato and Black Bean Quesadillas: 79

Mediterranean Chickpea Salad: 80

Butternut Squash and Sage Risotto: 81

Falafel Wraps with Tzatziki Sauce: 82

Maintaining the Mediterranean Diet for Long-Term Success 83

BONUS 85

30-Day Healthy Meal Plan 85

ENCOURAGEMENT

Dear Reader,

In the pursuit of lasting lifestyle changes, you are not just chasing a goal; you are sculpting a new way of living that resonates with your deepest desires for health and happiness. Change is a journey, and every step forward is a testament to your resilience and commitment.

Embrace Progress, Not Perfection: Remember, it's not about flawless execution but about progress. Celebrate the small victories—the days you choose nourishing meals, the moments you prioritize self-care, and the instances you choose positivity. These are the building blocks of lasting change.

Cultivate Self-Compassion: Be kind to yourself. Transformation is not linear; there will be setbacks and detours. Instead of dwelling on perceived failures, view them as opportunities to learn and adjust. Treat yourself with the same compassion you offer to your closest friends.

Discover Joy in the Journey: Lifestyle changes are not meant to be a burdensome task but a joyous exploration of self-discovery. Find pleasure in trying new recipes, in the endorphins released during a workout, and in the serenity of mindful moments. The journey itself holds the magic.

Forge Connections and Seek Support: Share your aspirations with others—family, friends, or a community on a similar journey. The support and shared experiences can fuel your motivation. Together, you create a network of encouragement that can weather challenges and celebrate triumphs.

Create a Vision, Not a Restriction: Envision the life you want to lead—one filled with vitality, fulfillment, and balance. Rather than focusing on restrictions, emphasize the abundance of choices that align with your vision. Your lifestyle is a canvas, and you hold the brush.

Nourish Your Mind and Body: Lifestyle changes extend beyond the physical; they encompass mental and emotional well-being. Prioritize activities that bring joy, practice mindfulness to quiet the mind, and surround yourself with positivity. A nourished mind supports a healthy body.

Seize the Power of Now: Every decision to prioritize health is a powerful act of self-love. Don't wait for a specific date or circumstance to start; the present moment is your canvas for change. Small, intentional choices today pave the way for a brighter, healthier tomorrow.

INTRODUCTION

In the bustling heart of a modern city, where the pace is relentless and stress is a daily companion, Emily found herself yearning for a change. Fueled by a desire to reclaim her well-being, she stumbled upon a culinary treasure trove that would not only transform her meals but her entire life. Little did she know, her journey to success would be written in the vibrant pages of this book.

As Emily opened the book, she entered a world where each recipe whispered promises of health, joy, and a profound connection to the art of living. At first, it was just a collection of enticing recipes, but as she explored the pages, she realized it was a roadmap to a life filled with vitality and flavor.

Armed with the culinary secrets of the Mediterranean, Emily began her gastronomic adventure, trading processed meals for vibrant salads kissed by the sun, savoring seafood dishes that danced on her taste buds, and relishing the robust flavors of olive oil, a golden elixir that became her kitchen muse.

The change was not just in the recipes; it was in the ritual of preparing and sharing meals. Emily discovered a newfound joy in the kitchen, transforming it from a place of mere function to a sanctuary of creativity and nourishment.

As she adopted the Mediterranean lifestyle, her energy soared, stress melted away, and the glow of well-being became her signature.

But Emily's success didn't stop at the kitchen. With newfound vitality, she embraced life's challenges with resilience. The harmonious dance of Mediterranean flavors spilled over into her work, relationships, and self-care rituals, shaping a success story that unfolded beyond the culinary realm.

This book wasn't just a cookbook for Emily; it was the catalyst for a life well-lived. As she savored each bite, she savored the victories, both big and small, that sprouted from her newfound zest for life. Emily's story is a testament to the transformative power of a cookbook – a narrative where success is not just measured in accomplishments but in the richness of every Mediterranean-inspired moment.

Overview, Health Benefits and Research Findings

The Mediterranean Diet, rooted in the rich culinary traditions of countries bordering the Mediterranean Sea, is more than just a way of eating; it's a lifestyle celebrated for its profound impact on health and well-being. Dating back centuries, this dietary pattern has captured the attention of nutritionists and researchers alike, garnering praise for its diverse range of nutrient-dense foods and association with numerous health benefits.

1. **Heart Health:**

- Numerous studies have shown that the Mediterranean diet is associated with a reduced risk of heart disease. The emphasis on olive oil, fish, nuts, and whole grains contributes to lower levels of bad cholesterol and improved cardiovascular health.

2. **Weight Management:**

- The Mediterranean diet is not just a short-term solution; it's a sustainable lifestyle for weight management. The abundance of fiber-rich fruits, vegetables, and whole grains promotes satiety, making it easier to maintain a healthy weight.

3. **Reduced Inflammation:**

- Rich in anti-inflammatory foods like fatty fish, nuts, and olive oil, the Mediterranean diet has been linked to lower levels of inflammatory markers. Chronic inflammation is associated with various health issues, including heart disease and certain cancers.

4. **Improved Cognitive Function:**

- Studies suggest that adherence to the Mediterranean diet is associated with better cognitive function and a lower risk of neurodegenerative diseases such as Alzheimer's. The combination of antioxidants and omega-3 fatty acids may play a protective role in brain health.

5. **Diabetes Prevention and Management:**

- Research indicates that the Mediterranean diet can be effective in preventing and managing type 2 diabetes. The emphasis on whole, unprocessed foods and healthy fats helps regulate blood sugar levels.

6. **Cancer Prevention:**

- Some studies suggest that the Mediterranean diet may have a protective effect against certain types of cancer, particularly colorectal and breast cancers. The abundance of antioxidants and fiber is believed to contribute to this benefit.

Research Findings:

1. PREDIMED Study:

- The PREDIMED (Prevención con Dieta Mediterránea) study, a landmark clinical trial, demonstrated that individuals following a Mediterranean diet supplemented with extra virgin olive oil or nuts had a significantly lower risk of major cardiovascular events compared to those following a low-fat diet.

2. Cognitive Function and Aging:

- Research published in the "Journal of the American Geriatrics Society" suggests that adherence to the Mediterranean diet is associated with a lower risk of cognitive decline as individuals age. The study linked the diet to better memory and overall cognitive performance.

3. Impact on Metabolic Syndrome:

- A meta-analysis published in the "Journal of the American College of Cardiology" found that the Mediterranean diet is effective in improving various components of metabolic syndrome, including waist circumference, blood pressure, and lipid levels.

4. Diabetes Prevention:

- The "Diabetes Care" journal published findings indicating that adopting a Mediterranean diet can reduce the risk of developing type 2 diabetes. The study emphasized the importance of the diet's composition in promoting metabolic health.

5. Longevity and Quality of Life:

- Studies conducted in Mediterranean regions, such as the "Blue Zones," where people live exceptionally long and healthy lives, attribute the residents' well-being to their dietary habits. The Mediterranean diet is a key factor in promoting longevity and an enhanced quality of life.

Emphasis on Whole, Unprocessed Foods

The essence of the Mediterranean diet lies in its unwavering emphasis on whole, unprocessed foods, echoing a return to the simplicity and purity of nature. This dietary philosophy recognizes that true nourishment comes from foods as close to their natural state as possible, celebrating the bounty of the earth and the richness of unadulterated flavors.

Abundance of Fresh Fruits and Vegetables:

The Mediterranean diet champions an abundance of colorful fruits and vegetables, a vibrant palette of nature's gifts. Packed with vitamins, minerals, and antioxidants, these whole foods contribute to optimal health and vitality.

Whole Grains as Dietary Staples:

Whole grains take center stage, with choices like brown rice, quinoa, and whole wheat bread offering a wholesome foundation. These grains retain their fiber and nutrients, promoting sustained energy levels and digestive well-being.

Heart-Healthy Olive Oil:

Olive oil, a cornerstone of the Mediterranean diet, exemplifies the essence of unprocessed goodness. Cold-pressed and rich in monounsaturated fats, it stands as a testament to the beauty of simplicity, elevating dishes with its natural aroma and flavor.

Lean Proteins from Natural Sources:

The diet favors lean proteins from unprocessed sources such as fish, poultry, legumes, and nuts. These protein-rich foods supply essential amino acids without the additives and preservatives often found in processed alternatives.

Dairy in Its Purest Form:

Dairy products, when included, are chosen in their most natural state. Greek yogurt, for instance, retains probiotics and nutrients, offering a wholesome addition to the diet without the excess sugars or artificial additives found in some commercial yogurts.

Minimally Processed Herbs and Spices:

The Mediterranean kitchen embraces a medley of herbs and spices, unprocessed and bursting with flavor. From the robust aroma of fresh basil to the warmth of oregano, these culinary treasures enhance meals without relying on excessive salt or artificial seasonings.

Nuts and Seeds for Nutrient Density:

Nuts and seeds, unsullied by processing, provide a nutrient-dense source of healthy fats, vitamins, and minerals. Whether sprinkled on salads or enjoyed as a snack, they exemplify the nutritional richness derived from nature's bounty.

Local and Seasonal Eating:

The Mediterranean approach celebrates local, seasonal eating, encouraging a connection to the land and a reduced reliance on processed and transported foods. Freshness and authenticity become guiding principles in every culinary creation.

Analysis of Key Nutrients and Their Impact on Health

1. **Monounsaturated Fats (MUFA):**

    - *Source:* Olive oil, nuts, and avocados.

    - *Impact:* MUFA is a heart-healthy fat that helps lower bad cholesterol (LDL) while maintaining or increasing good cholesterol (HDL). It contributes to cardiovascular health and has been associated with a reduced risk of heart disease.

2. **Omega-3 Fatty Acids:**

    - *Source:* Fatty fish (salmon, mackerel), walnuts, flaxseeds.

    - *Impact:* Omega-3 fatty acids are crucial for brain health, reducing inflammation, and supporting cardiovascular function. Regular consumption is linked to a lower risk of heart disease and improved cognitive function.

3. **Fiber:**

    - *Source:* Whole grains, fruits, vegetables, legumes.

    - *Impact:* The high fiber content in the Mediterranean diet promotes digestive health, regulates blood sugar levels, and contributes to satiety, aiding in weight management. It also lowers the risk of developing heart disease and supports a healthy gut microbiome.

4. **Antioxidants:**

    - *Source:* Colorful fruits and vegetables, herbs, spices.

    - *Impact:* Antioxidants, such as vitamins C and E, protect cells from damage caused by free radicals. They play a vital role in reducing inflammation, supporting the immune system, and are associated with a lower risk of chronic diseases.

5. **Lean Proteins:**

    - *Source:* Fish, poultry, legumes, nuts.

    - *Impact:* Lean protein sources in the Mediterranean diet provide essential amino acids for muscle health, immune function, and overall bodily repair. They contribute to a balanced diet without the drawbacks of excessive saturated fats found in some animal proteins.

6. **Vitamins and Minerals:**

    - *Source:* Fruits, vegetables, whole grains, nuts.

    - *Impact:* The diet is rich in vitamins and minerals such as vitamin A, vitamin C, potassium, and magnesium. These nutrients support various bodily functions, including immune health, bone health, and the maintenance of healthy skin.

7. **Polyphenols:**

    - *Source:* Red wine, tea, fruits, vegetables.

    - *Impact:* Polyphenols are powerful antioxidants with anti-inflammatory properties. They contribute to cardiovascular health, support brain function, and may play a role in preventing chronic diseases.

8. **Phytochemicals:**

    - *Source:* Garlic, onions, tomatoes.

    - *Impact:* Phytochemicals have been linked to cancer prevention and overall health. Garlic, for example, is known for its immune-boosting properties and potential to reduce the risk of certain cancers.

Food to Include, Limit and Avoid

Foods to Include:

1. **Fruits and Vegetables:**

   - Include a variety of colorful fruits and vegetables to ensure a wide range of nutrients and antioxidants.

   - Aim for at least 5 servings per day.

2. **Whole Grains:**

   - Choose whole grains such as brown rice, quinoa, oats, and whole wheat for fiber and essential nutrients.

3. **Lean Proteins:**

   - Include lean sources of protein such as poultry, fish, tofu, legumes, and beans.

   - Incorporate fish rich in omega-3 fatty acids for heart health.

4. **Healthy Fats:**

   - Include sources of healthy fats such as avocados, nuts, seeds, and olive oil.

   - Fatty fish like salmon and mackerel provide omega-3 fatty acids.

5. **Dairy or Dairy Alternatives:**

   - Choose low-fat or fat-free dairy products or fortified plant-based alternatives for calcium and vitamin D.

6. **Hydration:**

   - Drink plenty of water throughout the day to stay hydrated.

   - Herbal teas and infused water are good alternatives.

7. **Herbs and Spices:**

   - Use herbs and spices to add flavor to dishes without excessive salt or added sugars.

Foods to Avoid:

1. **Processed Foods:**

   - Limit the intake of processed foods, which often contain added sugars, unhealthy fats, and preservatives.

2. **Sugary Beverages:**

   - Avoid sugary drinks such as soda, energy drinks, and excessive fruit juices.

   - Opt for water, herbal teas, or naturally flavored water.

3. **Trans Fats:**

    - Avoid foods containing trans fats, often found in processed and fried foods.

    - Check food labels for hydrogenated or partially hydrogenated oils.

4. **Excessive Added Sugars:**

    - Minimize the consumption of foods high in added sugars, such as candies, pastries, and sugary cereals.

    - Choose whole fruits as a sweet treat.

5. **Highly Processed Meats:**

    - Limit processed meats like sausages, bacon, and hot dogs, which may contain preservatives and high levels of sodium.

6. **Refined Grains:**

    - Reduce the intake of refined grains like white bread, white rice, and sugary cereals.

    - Choose whole grains for higher nutritional value.

Foods to Limit:

1. **Sodium:**

   - Limit high-sodium foods like processed meats, canned soups, and salty snacks.
   - Choose low-sodium alternatives and use herbs and spices for flavor.

2. **Alcohol:**

   - Consume alcohol in moderation, if at all.
   - Moderation is generally defined as up to one drink per day for women and up to two drinks per day for men.

3. **Highly Caffeinated Beverages:**

   - Limit the intake of highly caffeinated beverages.
   - Choose moderate amounts of coffee and tea and avoid excessive energy drinks.

Delicious Breakfast Recipes

Greek Yogurt Parfait:

Ingredients:

- Greek yogurt
- Honey
- Granola
- Mixed berries
- Chopped nuts (optional)

Instructions:

1. In a glass or bowl, layer Greek yogurt.
2. Drizzle with honey and sprinkle granola.
3. Add a layer of mixed berries.
4. Repeat the layers and top with chopped nuts if desired.

Mediterranean Veggie Omelet:

Ingredients:

- Eggs
- Cherry tomatoes, halved
- Spinach
- Feta cheese
- Olive oil

Instructions:

1. Whisk eggs in a bowl.
2. In a skillet, sauté cherry tomatoes and spinach in olive oil.
3. Pour whisked eggs over the veggies, sprinkle feta, and cook until set.

Banana and Almond Butter Toast:

Ingredients:

- Whole grain bread
- Ripe banana, sliced
- Almond butter

Instructions:

1. Toast the whole grain bread.
2. Spread almond butter on the toast.
3. Arrange banana slices on top.

Spinach and Feta Breakfast Wrap:

Ingredients:

- Whole wheat tortilla
- Eggs, scrambled
- Fresh spinach
- Feta cheese

Instructions:

1. Fill a whole wheat tortilla halfway with scrambled eggs.
2. Add fresh spinach and crumbled feta.
3. Roll into a wrap.

Overnight Chia Seed Pudding:

Ingredients:

- Chia seeds
- Almond milk
- Greek yogurt
- Honey
- Fresh berries

Instructions:

1. Mix chia seeds, almond milk, and Greek yogurt in a jar.
2. Sweeten with honey and refrigerate overnight.
3. Top with fresh berries before serving.

Avocado and Smoked Salmon Bagel:

Ingredients:

- Whole grain bagel
- Ripe avocado
- Smoked salmon
- Lemon juice
- Capers (optional)

Instructions:

1. Toast the whole grain bagel.
2. Mash avocado and spread it on the bagel.
3. Top with smoked salmon, a squeeze of lemon juice, and capers if desired.

Mediterranean Frittata:

Ingredients:

- Eggs
- Cherry tomatoes, halved
- Kalamata olives, sliced
- Feta cheese
- Fresh oregano

Instructions:

1. Beat the eggs and place them into a greased baking dish.
2. Add halved cherry tomatoes, sliced olives, crumbled feta, and fresh oregano.
3. Bake until the eggs are set.

Blueberry and Almond Smoothie Bowl:

Ingredients:

- Frozen blueberries
- Almond milk
- Greek yogurt
- Almond butter
- Granola

Instructions:

1. Blend frozen blueberries, almond milk, Greek yogurt, and almond butter.
2. Place in a bowl and sprinkle with granola.

Whole Wheat Pancakes with Berries:

Ingredients:

- Whole wheat pancake mix
- Water or milk
- Mixed berries
- Maple syrup

Instructions:

1. Prepare whole wheat pancake batter according to the package instructions.
2. Cook pancakes and top with mixed berries and maple syrup.

Veggie and Cheese Breakfast Burrito:

Ingredients:

- Whole wheat tortilla
- Scrambled eggs
- Sautéed bell peppers and onions
- Shredded cheese
- Salsa

Instructions:

1. Fill a whole wheat tortilla with scrambled eggs, sautéed veggies, and shredded cheese.
2. Roll into a burrito and serve with salsa.

Sides Recipes

Tzatziki Sauce:

Ingredients:

- Greek yogurt
- Cucumber, grated and drained
- Garlic, minced
- Fresh dill, chopped
- Lemon juice
- Salt and pepper to taste

Instructions:

1. Combine Greek yogurt, grated cucumber, minced garlic, chopped dill, and lemon juice in a mixing bowl.
2. Season with salt and pepper. Refrigerate before serving.

Roasted Garlic and Rosemary Potatoes:

Ingredients:

- Baby potatoes, halved
- Olive oil
- Garlic, minced
- Fresh rosemary, chopped
- Salt and pepper to taste

Instructions:

1. Toss halved baby potatoes with olive oil, minced garlic, and chopped rosemary.
2. Season with salt and pepper, then roast until golden brown.

Greek Salad:

Ingredients:

- Cucumbers, diced
- Tomatoes, diced
- Red onion, thinly sliced
- Kalamata olives
- Feta cheese, crumbled
- Olive oil
- Red wine vinegar
- Oregano, dried or fresh
- Salt and pepper to taste

Instructions:

1. Combine cucumbers, tomatoes, red onion, olives, and feta in a bowl.
2. Drizzle with olive oil and red wine vinegar, sprinkle with oregano, salt, and pepper. Toss gently.

Lemon Garlic Quinoa:

Ingredients:

- Quinoa
- Vegetable broth
- Lemon juice
- Garlic, minced
- Olive oil
- Salt and pepper to taste

Instructions:

1. Cook the quinoa in the veggie broth according to the package directions.
2. Fluff with a fork and toss with lemon juice, minced garlic, olive oil, salt, and pepper.

Caprese Skewers:

Ingredients:

- Cherry tomatoes
- Fresh mozzarella balls
- Basil leaves
- Balsamic glaze
- Salt and pepper to taste

Instructions:

1. Skewers should be threaded with cherry tomatoes, mozzarella balls, and basil leaves.
2. Drizzle with balsamic glaze, sprinkle with salt and pepper.

Spinach and Feta Stuffed Mushrooms:

Ingredients:

- Mushrooms, cleaned and stems removed
- Spinach, chopped
- Feta cheese, crumbled
- Garlic, minced
- Olive oil
- Breadcrumbs
- Salt and pepper to taste

Instructions:

1. Sauté chopped spinach and minced garlic in olive oil.
2. Mix with feta, stuff into mushrooms, sprinkle with breadcrumbs, and bake until mushrooms are tender.

Grilled Asparagus with Lemon Zest:

Ingredients:

- Fresh asparagus spears
- Olive oil
- Lemon zest
- Salt and pepper to taste

Instructions:

1. Toss the asparagus spears with the olive oil, lemon zest, salt, and pepper to taste.
2. Grill until asparagus is tender and slightly charred.

Eggplant Caponata:

Ingredients:

- Eggplant, diced
- Tomatoes, diced
- Celery, diced
- Red bell pepper, diced
- Red onion, diced
- Garlic, minced
- Olive oil
- Red wine vinegar
- Capers
- Olives, chopped
- Fresh basil, chopped
- Salt and pepper to taste

Instructions:

1. Sauté diced eggplant, tomatoes, celery, red bell pepper, and red onion in olive oil.
2. Add minced garlic, red wine vinegar, capers, chopped olives, and fresh basil.
3. Season with salt and pepper.

Quinoa Tabbouleh:

Ingredients:

- Quinoa, cooked
- Fresh parsley, chopped
- Tomatoes, diced

- Cucumber, diced
- Red onion, finely chopped
- Lemon juice
- Olive oil
- Salt and pepper to taste

Instructions:

1. Combine cooked quinoa with chopped parsley, diced tomatoes, cucumber, and red onion.
2. Dress with lemon juice, olive oil, salt, and pepper.

Mediterranean Roasted Vegetables:

- Ingredients:
- Bell peppers, sliced
- Zucchini, sliced
- Red onion, sliced
- Cherry tomatoes
- Garlic, minced
- Olive oil Fresh thyme, chopped
- Salt and pepper to taste

- Instructions:

1. Toss sliced bell peppers, zucchini, red onion, and cherry tomatoes with minced garlic in olive oil.

2. Sprinkle with fresh thyme, salt, and pepper. Roast until vegetables are tender and caramelized.

Main Courses

Lemon Herb Grilled Chicken:

Ingredients:

- Chicken breasts
- Lemon juice
- Olive oil
- Garlic, minced
- Fresh thyme, chopped
- Salt and pepper

Instructions:

1. In a bowl, mix lemon juice, olive oil, minced garlic, chopped thyme, salt, and pepper.
2. Marinate chicken breasts in the mixture and grill until fully cooked.

Mediterranean Baked Cod:

Ingredients:

- Cod fillets
- Cherry tomatoes, halved
- Kalamata olives, sliced
- Red onion, thinly sliced

- Garlic, minced
- Olive oil
- Fresh basil, chopped
- Lemon wedges

Instructions:

1. Place cod fillets in a baking dish.
2. Top with cherry tomatoes, olives, red onion, and minced garlic. Drizzle with olive oil.
3. Bake until the cod is flaky. Serve with lemon wedges and garnished with fresh basil.

Eggplant Parmesan:

Ingredients:

- Eggplant, sliced
- Marinara sauce
- Mozzarella cheese, shredded
- Parmesan cheese, grated
- Fresh basil, chopped
- Olive oil
- Salt and pepper

Instructions:

1. Layer sliced eggplant with marinara sauce, mozzarella, and Parmesan in a baking dish.
2. Bake until the cheese is melted and bubbly. Garnish with fresh basil.

Mediterranean Shrimp and Orzo Salad:

Ingredients:

- Shrimp, peeled and deveined
- Orzo pasta
- Cherry tomatoes, halved
- Cucumber, diced
- Feta cheese, crumbled
- Kalamata olives, sliced
- Olive oil
- Lemon juice
- Fresh dill, chopped

Instructions:

1. Cook orzo pasta and grill shrimp.
2. Mix orzo with cherry tomatoes, cucumber, feta, olives, olive oil, lemon

Chicken Souvlaki Skewers:

Ingredients

- Chicken thighs, cut into cubes
- Olive oil
- Lemon juice
- Garlic, minced
- Oregano, dried or fresh
- Red onion, sliced
- Tzatziki sauce (for serving)

Instructions:

1. In a bowl, mix olive oil, lemon juice, minced garlic, and oregano.
2. Marinate chicken cubes in the mixture and thread onto skewers with red onion slices.
3. Grill until the chicken is cooked through. Serve with tzatziki sauce.

Lentil and Vegetable Moussaka:

Ingredients:

- Lentils, cooked
- Eggplant, sliced
- Zucchini, sliced
- Red bell pepper, diced

- Onion, chopped
- Garlic, minced
- Tomato sauce
- Olive oil
- Cinnamon, ground
- Nutmeg, ground
- Feta cheese, crumbled

Instructions:

1. Sauté onions and garlic in olive oil. Add lentils, diced vegetables, tomato sauce, cinnamon, and nutmeg.
2. Layer the lentil mixture with sliced eggplant and zucchini in a baking dish. Top with crumbled feta.
3. Bake until vegetables are tender and the top is golden.

Spinach and Feta Stuffed Chicken Breast:

Ingredients:

- **Chicken breasts**
- **Spinach, chopped**
- **Feta cheese, crumbled**
- **Garlic, minced**
- Olive oil
- Lemon juice

- Salt and pepper

Instructions:

1. Preheat the oven. Season the chicken breasts with salt and pepper and butterfly them. Sauté chopped spinach and garlic in olive oil. Mix with crumbled feta.
2. Stuff the chicken breasts with the spinach and feta mixture. Drizzle with lemon juice.
3. Bake until chicken is cooked through.

Grilled Vegetable and Halloumi Skewers:

Ingredients:

- Halloumi cheese, cubed
- Cherry tomatoes
- Zucchini, sliced
- Red bell pepper, diced
- Olive oil
- Lemon juice
- Oregano, dried or fresh
- Salt and pepper

Instructions:

1. Thread halloumi cubes, cherry tomatoes, zucchini, and red bell pepper onto skewers.
2. Mix olive oil, lemon juice, oregano, salt, and pepper. Brush over skewers.
3. Grill until the halloumi is golden and vegetables are tender.

Pasta Puttanesca

Ingredients:

- Spaghetti
- Canned tomatoes
- Kalamata olives, sliced
- Capers
- Anchovies, chopped (optional)
- Garlic, minced
- Olive oil
- Red pepper flakes
- Fresh parsley, chopped

Instructions:

1. Cook spaghetti according to package instructions.
2. Sauté garlic in olive oil, add canned tomatoes, olives, capers, and anchovies. Simmer.

3. Toss cooked spaghetti in the sauce. Serve with red pepper flakes and fresh parsley as garnish.

Stuffed Bell Peppers with Quinoa and Chickpeas:

Ingredients:

- Bell peppers, halved
- Quinoa, cooked
- Chickpeas, cooked
- Cherry tomatoes, diced
- Feta cheese, crumbled
- Olive oil
- Lemon juice
- Fresh mint, chopped
- Salt and pepper

Instructions:

1. Preheat the oven. Mix cooked quinoa, chickpeas, diced tomatoes, crumbled feta, olive oil, lemon juice, chopped mint, salt, and pepper.

2. Stuff halved bell peppers with the quinoa mixture. Bake until peppers are tender.

Appetizers and Snacks Recipes

Hummus and Veggie Platter:

Ingredients:

- Hummus
- Baby carrots
- Cucumber slices
- Cherry tomatoes
- Bell pepper strips

Instructions:

1. Arrange a variety of vegetables around a bowl of hummus for dipping.

Caprese Skewers:

Ingredients:

- Cherry tomatoes
- Fresh mozzarella balls
- Basil leaves
- Balsamic glaze

Instructions:

1. Skewers should be threaded with cherry tomatoes, mozzarella balls, and basil leaves.
2. Drizzle with balsamic glaze.

Greek Spanakopita Triangles:

- **Ingredients:**
- Phyllo dough
- Spinach, chopped
- Feta cheese, crumbled
- Onion, finely chopped
- Olive oil

Instructions:

1. Mix chopped spinach, crumbled feta, and finely chopped onion.
2. Place spoonfuls of the mixture on phyllo dough, fold into triangles, and bake until golden.

Tomato Bruschetta:

Ingredients:

- Baguette slices
- Tomatoes, diced
- Fresh basil, chopped
- Garlic, minced

- Olive oil
- Balsamic vinegar
- Salt and pepper

Instructions:

1. Toast baguette slices.
2. Mix diced tomatoes, chopped basil, minced garlic, olive oil, balsamic vinegar, salt, and pepper. Spoon onto the toasted baguette slices.

Stuffed Grape Leaves (Dolma):

Ingredients:

- Grape leaves
- Rice
- Pine nuts
- Currants
- Fresh dill, chopped
- Lemon juice
- Olive oil

Instructions:

1. Mix cooked rice with pine nuts, currants, chopped dill, lemon juice, and olive oil.
2. Wrap the mixture in grape leaves and steam until cooked.

Greek Yogurt and Cucumber Dip:

Ingredients:

- Greek yogurt
- Cucumber, finely diced
- Garlic, minced
- Fresh dill, chopped
- Lemon juice
- Salt and pepper

Instructions:

1. Combine Greek yogurt, diced cucumber, minced garlic, chopped dill, lemon juice, salt, and pepper. Mix well.

Olive Tapenade:

Ingredients:

- Kalamata olives, pitted
- Capers
- Garlic, minced
- Fresh parsley, chopped
- Lemon juice
- Olive oil

Instructions:

1. Blend olives, capers, minced garlic, chopped parsley, lemon juice, and olive oil until chunky.

Baked Feta with Honey and Nuts:

Ingredients:

- Feta cheese
- Honey
- Walnuts, chopped

Instructions:

1. Place a block of feta in a baking dish, drizzle with honey, and sprinkle chopped walnuts.
2. Bake until the feta is soft and slightly golden.

Mediterranean Bruschetta:

Ingredients:

- Tomatoes, diced
- Red onion, finely chopped
- Kalamata olives, chopped
- Fresh basil, chopped
- Olive oil
- Balsamic glaze

- Salt and pepper

Instructions:

1. Mix diced tomatoes, chopped red onion, olives, and basil.
2. Drizzle with olive oil and balsamic glaze. Season with salt and pepper. Spoon onto toasted baguette slices.

Spicy Roasted Chickpeas:

Ingredients:

- Canned chickpeas, drained and rinsed
- Olive oil
- Smoked paprika
- Cumin
- Cayenne pepper
- Salt

Instructions:

1. Toss chickpeas with olive oil, smoked paprika, cumin, cayenne pepper, and salt.
2. Roast in the oven until crispy.

Salads and Soup Recipes

Greek Salad:

Ingredients:

- Cucumbers, diced
- Tomatoes, diced
- Red onion, thinly sliced
- Kalamata olives
- Feta cheese, crumbled
- Olive oil
- Red wine vinegar
- Oregano, dried or fresh
- Salt and pepper

Instructions:

1. Combine cucumbers, tomatoes, red onion, olives, and feta in a bowl.
2. Drizzle with olive oil and red wine vinegar. Sprinkle with oregano, salt, and pepper. Toss gently.

Quinoa Salad with Chickpeas and Lemon Vinaigrette:

Ingredients:

- Quinoa, cooked
- Chickpeas, cooked
- Cherry tomatoes, halved
- Cucumber, diced
- Red bell pepper, diced
- Red onion, finely chopped
- Feta cheese, crumbled
- Fresh parsley, chopped
- Olive oil
- Lemon juice
- Salt and pepper

Instructions:

1. In a large bowl, combine cooked quinoa, chickpeas, tomatoes, cucumber, red bell pepper, red onion, feta, and parsley.
2. Drizzle with olive oil and lemon juice. Season with salt and pepper. Toss to combine.

Mediterranean Chickpea Salad:

Ingredients:

- Canned chickpeas, drained and rinsed
- Cherry tomatoes, halved
- Cucumber, diced
- Red onion, finely chopped
- Feta cheese, crumbled
- Kalamata olives
- Olive oil
- Red wine vinegar
- Oregano, dried or fresh
- Salt and pepper

Instructions:

1. In a large bowl, combine chickpeas, tomatoes, cucumber, red onion, feta, and olives.
2. Drizzle with olive oil and red wine vinegar. Sprinkle with oregano, salt, and pepper. Toss gently.

Lentil and Vegetable Soup:

Ingredients:

- Lentils, rinsed and drained
- Carrots, diced
- Celery, diced
- Onion, finely chopped
- Garlic, minced
- Tomatoes, diced
- Vegetable broth
- Olive oil
- Cumin
- Coriander
- Bay leaves
- Salt and pepper

Instructions:

1. In a pot, sauté onion, garlic, carrots, and celery in olive oil until softened.
2. Add lentils, tomatoes, vegetable broth, cumin, coriander, bay leaves, salt, and pepper. Simmer until lentils are tender.

Fattoush Salad:

Ingredients:

- Romaine lettuce, chopped
- Cucumber, diced
- Tomatoes, diced
- Radishes, sliced
- Red onion, thinly sliced
- Fresh mint, chopped
- Pita bread, toasted and broken into pieces
- Sumac
- Olive oil
- Lemon juice
- Salt and pepper

Instructions:

1. In a large bowl, combine lettuce, cucumber, tomatoes, radishes, red onion, mint, and toasted pita pieces.
2. Drizzle with olive oil and lemon juice. Sprinkle with sumac, salt, and pepper. Toss gently.

Minestrone Soup:

Ingredients:

- Onion, diced
- Carrots, diced
- Celery, diced
- Zucchini, diced
- Canned tomatoes, diced
- Kidney beans, drained and rinsed
- Cannellini beans, drained and rinsed
- Vegetable broth
- Pasta
- Olive oil
- Garlic, minced
- Basil, dried or fresh
- Salt and pepper

Instructions:

1. In a pot, sauté onion, carrots, celery, and zucchini in olive oil until softened.
2. Add garlic, diced tomatoes, kidney beans, cannellini beans, vegetable broth, pasta, and basil. Simmer until pasta is cooked. Season with salt and pepper.

Tabbouleh Salad:

Ingredients:

- Bulgur wheat, soaked and drained
- Fresh parsley, chopped
- Tomatoes, diced
- Cucumber, diced
- Green onions, chopped
- Fresh mint, chopped
- Olive oil
- Lemon juice
- Salt and pepper

Instructions:

1. In a bowl, combine soaked bulgur, parsley, tomatoes, cucumber, green onions, and mint.
2. Drizzle with olive oil and lemon juice. Season with salt and pepper. Toss gently.

Gazpacho:

Ingredients:

- Tomatoes, diced
- Cucumber, diced
- Bell pepper, diced
- Red onion, finely chopped
- Garlic, minced
- Tomato juice
- Olive oil
- Red wine vinegar
- Bread, crust removed
- Salt and pepper
- Fresh basil, chopped (for garnish)

Instructions:

1. In a blender, combine tomatoes, cucumber, bell pepper, red onion, garlic, tomato juice, olive oil, red wine vinegar, and bread. Blend until smooth.
2. Season with salt and pepper. Chill in the refrigerator. Before serving, sprinkle with fresh basil.

Cretan Dakos Salad:

Ingredients:

- Barley rusks or whole-grain bread
- Tomatoes, diced
- Feta cheese, crumbled
- Kalamata olives, sliced
- Olive oil
- Oregano, dried or fresh
- Salt and pepper

Instructions:

1. Place barley rusks or toasted whole-grain bread on a plate.
2. Top with diced tomatoes, crumbled feta, and sliced Kalamata olives. Drizzle with olive oil. Sprinkle with oregano, salt, and pepper.

Lemon Chickpea Orzo Soup:

Ingredients:

- Orzo pasta
- Canned chickpeas, drained and rinsed
- Spinach, chopped
- Lemon juice
- Vegetable broth

- Garlic, minced
- Olive oil
- Fresh dill, chopped
- Salt and pepper

Instructions:

1. Cook orzo according to package instructions.
2. In a pot, sauté garlic in olive oil. Add vegetable broth, chickpeas, cooked orzo, chopped spinach, and lemon juice. Simmer until heated through.
3. Season with salt and pepper. Garnish with fresh dill.

Dessert Recipes

Greek Yogurt and Honey Parfait:

Ingredients:

- Greek yogurt
- Honey
- Fresh berries (strawberries, blueberries, raspberries)
- Granola

Instructions:

1. In a glass or bowl, layer Greek yogurt, fresh berries, and granola.
2. Drizzle with honey. Repeat the layers for a delicious parfait.

Mediterranean Orange and Almond Cake:

Ingredients:

- Almond flour
- Oranges
- Eggs
- Honey
- Baking powder

Instructions:

1. Boil and puree whole oranges (including peel).
2. Mix with almond flour, eggs, honey, and baking powder.
3. Bake till a toothpick inserted into the center comes out clean. Dust with powdered sugar if desired.

Baklava:

Ingredients:

- Phyllo dough
- Walnuts or pistachios, chopped
- Butter, melted
- Sugar
- Cinnamon
- Honey

Instructions:

1. Layer phyllo dough, brushing each layer with melted butter.
2. Mix chopped nuts with sugar and cinnamon. Sprinkle over layers.
3. Bake until golden brown. Pour honey over the hot baklava.

Italian Tiramisu:

Ingredients:

- Ladyfingers
- Espresso
- Mascarpone cheese
- Eggs
- Sugar
- Cocoa powder

Instructions:

1. Dip ladyfingers in espresso and layer in a dish.
2. Mix mascarpone, egg yolks, and sugar. Spread over ladyfingers.
3. Whisk the egg whites until stiff peaks form, and then fold them into the mascarpone mixture.
4. Dust with cocoa powder. Refrigerate before serving.

Lemon Sorbet:

Ingredients:

- Lemons, juiced and zested
- Sugar
- Water

Instructions:

1. Dissolve sugar in water to make a simple syrup.
2. Mix with lemon juice and zest.
3. Freeze in an ice cream maker. Garnish with lemon zest.

Fig and Walnut Phyllo Rolls:

Ingredients:

- Dried figs, chopped
- Walnuts, chopped
- Honey
- Phyllo dough
- Butter, melted

Instructions:

1. Mix chopped figs and walnuts. Lay out phyllo sheets, brush with melted butter, and layer.
2. Spread the fig and walnut mixture. Roll into a log.
3. Bake until golden. Drizzle with honey.

Orange Blossom Panna Cotta:

Ingredients:

- Heavy cream
- Gelatin
- Sugar
- Orange blossom water
- Orange zest

Instructions:

1. Heat cream with sugar, gelatin, and orange zest.
2. Remove from heat, add orange blossom water. Pour into molds.
3. Refrigerate until set. Serve chilled.

Ricotta and Honey Stuffed Figs:

Ingredients:

- Fresh figs
- Ricotta cheese
- Honey
- Pistachios, chopped (optional)

Instructions:

1. Cut figs in half. Mix ricotta with honey.
2. Spoon ricotta mixture onto fig halves.

Drizzle with additional honey and top with chopped pistachios.

Chocolate Olive Oil Cake:

Ingredients:

- All-purpose flour
- Cocoa powder
- Baking powder
- Sugar
- Eggs
- Olive oil
- Vanilla extract
- Salt

Instructions:

1. Mix flour, cocoa, baking powder, and salt.
2. In another bowl, beat eggs, sugar, olive oil, and vanilla.
3. Combine wet and dry ingredients. Bake till a toothpick inserted into the center comes out clean.
4.

Lemon and Lavender Shortbread Cookies:

Ingredients:

- Butter
- Sugar
- All-purpose flour
- Lemon zest
- Dried lavender

Instructions:

1. Cream butter and sugar. Mix in flour, lemon zest, and dried lavender.
2. Roll into a log, chill, and slice. Bake until edges are golden.

Smoothies Recipes

Berry Blast Smoothie:

Ingredients:

- Mixed berries (strawberries, blueberries, raspberries)
- Banana
- Greek yogurt
- Honey
- Almond milk

Instructions:

1. Blend mixed berries, banana, Greek yogurt, honey, and almond milk until smooth.

Green Tropical Smoothie:

Ingredients:

- Spinach
- Pineapple chunks
- Mango chunks
- Banana
- Coconut water

Instructions:

1. Blend spinach, pineapple, mango, banana, and coconut water until well combined.

Peanut Butter Banana Protein Smoothie:

Ingredients:

- Banana
- Peanut butter
- Protein powder (vanilla or chocolate)
- Almond milk
- Ice cubes

Instructions:

1. Blend banana, peanut butter, protein powder, almond milk, and ice cubes until creamy.

Citrus Sunshine Smoothie:

Ingredients:

- Oranges, peeled and segmented
- Pineapple chunks
- Greek yogurt
- Honey

- Ice cubes

Instructions:

1. Blend oranges, pineapple, Greek yogurt, honey, and ice cubes for a zesty and refreshing smoothie.

Avocado and Kale Power Smoothie:

Ingredients:

- Avocado
- Kale leaves, stems removed
- Banana
- Chia seeds
- Coconut water

Instructions:

1. Blend avocado, kale, banana, chia seeds, and coconut water for a nutrient-packed smoothie.

Mango Coconut Bliss Smoothie:

Ingredients:

- Mango chunks
- Coconut milk
- Greek yogurt

- Shredded coconut
- Lime juice

Instructions:

1. Blend mango, coconut milk, Greek yogurt, shredded coconut, and lime juice for a tropical treat.

Blueberry Almond Spinach Smoothie:

Ingredients:

- Blueberries
- Spinach
- Almond butter
- Almond milk
- Flaxseeds

Instructions:

1. Blend blueberries, spinach, almond butter, almond milk, and flaxseeds for a nutrient-rich smoothie.

Watermelon Mint Cooler Smoothie:

Ingredients:

- Watermelon chunks
- Mint leaves
- Cucumber, peeled and sliced
- Lime juice
- Coconut water

Instructions:

1. Blend watermelon, mint, cucumber, lime juice, and coconut water for a hydrating and refreshing smoothie.

Chocolate Banana Almond Smoothie:

Ingredients:

- Banana
- Almond butter
- Cocoa powder
- Almond milk
- Ice cubes

Instructions:

1. Blend banana, almond butter, cocoa powder, almond milk, and ice cubes for a chocolatey delight.

Pineapple Ginger Turmeric Smoothie:

Ingredients:

- Pineapple chunks
- Fresh ginger, grated
- Turmeric powder
- Greek yogurt
- Coconut water

Instructions:

1. Blend pineapple, grated ginger, turmeric powder, Greek yogurt, and coconut water for a tropical and anti-inflammatory smoothie.

Vegetarian Recipes

Quinoa Stuffed Bell Peppers:

Ingredients:

- Bell peppers, halved
- Quinoa, cooked
- Black beans, drained and rinsed
- Corn kernels
- Diced tomatoes
- Red onion, finely chopped
- Mexican spices (cumin, chili powder, paprika)
- Shredded cheese

Instructions:

1. Preheat the oven. Mix cooked quinoa with black beans, corn, diced tomatoes, red onion, and spices.
2. Stuff bell peppers with the quinoa mixture. Top with shredded cheese.
3. Bake until peppers are tender and cheese is melted.

Eggplant Parmesan:

Ingredients:

- Eggplant, sliced
- Marinara sauce
- Mozzarella cheese, shredded
- Parmesan cheese, grated
- Fresh basil, chopped
- Olive oil
- Salt and pepper

Instructions:

1. Layer sliced eggplant with marinara sauce, mozzarella, and Parmesan in a baking dish.
2. Bake until the cheese is melted and bubbly. Garnish with fresh basil.

Lentil and Vegetable Stir-Fry:

Ingredients:

- Lentils, cooked
- Mixed vegetables (broccoli, bell peppers, snap peas)
- Garlic, minced
- Soy sauce
- Sesame oil

- Ginger, grated
- Green onions, sliced

Instructions:

1. Stir-fry mixed vegetables with garlic, ginger, and cooked lentils in sesame oil and soy sauce.
2. Garnish with sliced green onions.

Spinach and Feta Stuffed Mushrooms:

Ingredients:

- Mushrooms, cleaned and stems removed
- Spinach, chopped
- Feta cheese, crumbled
- Garlic, minced
- Olive oil
- Bread crumbs

Instructions:

1. Sauté chopped spinach and garlic in olive oil. Mix with crumbled feta.
2. Stuff mushroom caps with the spinach and feta mixture. Sprinkle with bread crumbs.
3. Bake until mushrooms are tender.

Chickpea and Vegetable Curry:

Ingredients:

- Chickpeas, cooked
- Mixed vegetables (carrots, peas, potatoes)
- Onion, finely chopped
- Tomato, diced
- Coconut milk
- Curry spices (turmeric, cumin, coriander)
- Garlic, minced

Instructions:

1. Sauté onion and garlic in a pot. Add diced tomatoes and curry spices.
2. Add cooked chickpeas, mixed vegetables, and coconut milk. Simmer until vegetables are tender.

Caprese Pasta Salad:

Ingredients:

- Pasta (penne or fusilli)
- Cherry tomatoes, halved
- Fresh mozzarella, diced
- Fresh basil, chopped
- Balsamic glaze
- Olive oil
- Salt and pepper

Instructions:

1. Cook pasta according to package instructions.
2. Toss cooked pasta with cherry tomatoes, fresh mozzarella, and chopped basil.
3. Drizzle with olive oil and balsamic glaze. Season with salt and pepper.

Sweet Potato and Black Bean Quesadillas:

Ingredients:

- Sweet potatoes, cooked and mashed
- Black beans, mashed
- Tortillas
- Shredded cheddar cheese

- Cilantro, chopped
- Lime wedges

Instructions:

1. Spread mashed sweet potatoes and black beans on one half of a tortilla.
2. Sprinkle with shredded cheddar cheese and cilantro. Fold in half.
3. Cook on a skillet until the tortilla is crispy. Serve with lime wedges.

Mediterranean Chickpea Salad:

Ingredients:

- Canned chickpeas, drained and rinsed
- Cherry tomatoes, halved
- Cucumber, diced
- Red onion, finely chopped
- Feta cheese, crumbled
- Kalamata olives
- Olive oil
- Red wine vinegar
- Oregano, dried or fresh
- Salt and pepper

Instructions:

1. In a large bowl, combine chickpeas, tomatoes, cucumber, red onion, feta, and olives.
2. Drizzle with olive oil and red wine vinegar. Sprinkle with oregano, salt, and pepper. Toss gently.

Butternut Squash and Sage Risotto:

Ingredients:

- Arborio rice
- Butternut squash, diced
- Vegetable broth
- Onion, finely chopped
- White wine
- Parmesan cheese, grated
- Fresh sage, chopped
- Olive oil

Instructions:

1. Sauté chopped onion in olive oil. Add Arborio rice and diced butternut squash.
2. Deglaze with white wine. Stir in the veggie broth gradually until the rice is tender
3. Stir in grated Parmesan and chopped sage.

Falafel Wraps with Tzatziki Sauce:

Ingredients:

- Falafel patties (store-bought or homemade)
- Whole wheat wraps
- Cherry tomatoes, halved
- Cucumber, thinly sliced
- Red onion, thinly sliced
- Lettuce, shredded
- Tzatziki sauce

Instructions:

1. Heat falafel patties according to package instructions.
2. Assemble wraps with falafel, cherry tomatoes, cucumber, red onion, shredded lettuce, and a generous drizzle of tzatziki sauce.

Maintaining the Mediterranean Diet for Long-Term Success

1. **Culinary Creativity:** Explore diverse recipes and experiment with Mediterranean-inspired dishes to keep your meals exciting and satisfying.

2. **Social Connection:** Embrace the Mediterranean tradition of communal dining. Share meals with friends and family to foster a sense of community and joy around the table.

3. **Seasonal Variety:** Align your diet with seasonal produce for freshness and flavor. Embrace the changing availability of fruits, vegetables, and herbs to keep your meals dynamic.

4. **Mindful Eating:** Practice mindful eating by savoring each bite and paying attention to hunger and fullness cues. Enjoy the sensory experience of your meals.

5. **Regular Physical Activity:** Combine the Mediterranean diet with regular exercise to promote overall well-being. Engage in activities you enjoy, whether it's a scenic walk or a dance class.

6. **Hydration:** Stay well-hydrated with water and herbal teas. Limit sugary and high-calorie beverages, opting for refreshing and natural choices.

7. **Balanced Indulgences:** Allow yourself occasional indulgences without guilt. Enjoy a piece of dark chocolate or a small glass of red wine in moderation.

8. **Smart Substitutions:** Make healthier choices by swapping ingredients without sacrificing flavor. Choose whole grains, lean proteins, and healthy fats in your culinary endeavors.

9. **Educational Resources:** Stay informed about the latest research and insights into the Mediterranean diet. Keep learning and adapting your approach based on evolving nutritional knowledge.

10. **Lifestyle Integration:** Infuse the Mediterranean lifestyle into your daily routine beyond just meals. Prioritize stress management, sufficient sleep, and a positive mindset for holistic well-being.

BONUS

30-Day Healthy Meal Plan

Day	Breakfast	Lunch	Dinner
1	Scrambled Eggs with Spinach	Quinoa Salad with Chickpeas	Grilled Chicken Breast with Roasted Vegetables
2	Greek Yogurt Parfait	Turkey and Avocado Wrap	Baked Salmon with Quinoa
3	Oatmeal with Berries	Lentil Soup	Spaghetti Bolognese
4	Whole Grain Pancakes	Caprese Salad	Grilled Shrimp Tacos with Slaw
5	Smoothie with Kale and Banana	Chickpea and Quinoa Bowl	Teriyaki Tofu Stir-Fry
6	Chia Seed Pudding	Turkey and Hummus Sandwich	Eggplant Parmesan
7	Whole Wheat Toast with Avocado	Caesar Salad with Grilled Chicken	Baked Cod with Sweet Potato
8	Banana Walnut Muffins	Spinach and Feta Omelette	Vegetable Stir-Fry with Brown Rice

Day	Breakfast	Lunch	Dinner
9	Cottage Cheese with Pineapple	Quinoa and Black Bean Bowl	Grilled Turkey Burgers
10	Blueberry Smoothie Bowl	Chicken Caesar Wrap	Shrimp and Vegetable Skewers
11	Avocado Toast with Poached Eggs	Lentil and Vegetable Curry	Margherita Pizza
12	Peanut Butter Banana Toast	Greek Salad with Hummus	Baked Chicken with Sweet Potato
13	Yogurt with Mixed Berries	Chickpea and Avocado Salad	Quinoa-Stuffed Bell Peppers
14	Scrambled Tofu Breakfast Burrito	Turkey Club Sandwich	Mediterranean Lentil Soup
15	Overnight Chia Seed Pudding	Caprese Sandwich	Lemon Herb Grilled Chicken
16	Apple Cinnamon Oatmeal	Greek Gyro Salad	Spaghetti Aglio e Olio
17	Protein Smoothie with Berries	Quinoa and Chickpea Buddha Bowl	Baked Cod with Lemon Butter Sauce
18	Whole Grain Waffles with Fruit	Chicken and Vegetable Wrap	Stir-Fried Tofu with Broccoli

Day	Breakfast	Lunch	Dinner
19	Greek Yogurt with Granola	Lentil and Vegetable Stir-Fry	Grilled Salmon with Asparagus
20	Breakfast Burrito with Black Beans	Caprese Pasta Salad	Mediterranean Chickpea Salad
21	Veggie Omelette	Turkey and Quinoa Stuffed Peppers	Shrimp Scampi
22	Spinach and Mushroom Frittata	Quinoa Salad with Avocado	Teriyaki Chicken with Brown Rice
23	Mixed Berry Smoothie	Chicken Caesar Salad	Baked Zucchini Boats
24	Almond Butter Toast with Banana	Chickpea and Spinach Curry	Grilled Vegetable Quesadillas
25	Yogurt Parfait with Nuts	Turkey Club Wrap	Lemon Garlic Shrimp Linguine
26	Blueberry Pancakes	Mediterranean Hummus Bowl	Quinoa-Stuffed Portobello Mushrooms
27	Avocado and Tomato Toast	Lentil Soup	Baked Chicken Parmesan
28	Banana Walnut Smoothie Bowl	Greek Salad with Chicken	Vegetable Stir-Fry with Tofu
29	Scrambled Eggs with Tomatoes	Caprese Quinoa Bowl	Grilled Steak with Roasted Vegetables

Day	Breakfast	Lunch	Dinner
30	Chia Seed Pudding with Berries	Chicken and Vegetable Stir-Fry	Baked Cod with Mediterranean Salsa

Feel free to adapt this plan based on your taste preferences and dietary needs. Adjust portion sizes and ingredients as necessary to meet your nutritional requirement

Made in the USA
Coppell, TX
14 August 2024